From a New Forest Inclosure

Book Three 2008 & 2009

By

Ian Thew

Published by Burley Rails Publishing
Burley Rails Cottage BH24 4HT

ISBN 978-0-9570835-2-3

Ian Thew

Born in Southampton, Ian and his siblings were brought, throughout their childhood, into the New Forest to walk and enjoy the open space. Although, initially, he spent his adult life living and working away from the Forest he was always keen on the countryside and country sports, especially fishing and shooting. He returned whenever he could to the Forest until, eventually, he settled down in Burley with his late wife, Diane. In 1994 they moved to the remote Burley Rails Cottage which, originally built as a woodman's cottage and sold by the Forestry Commission in the 1960's, is a unique place in which to live.

Ian's knowledge of the forest is genuine and he is respected for his considerate and well researched articles which are published in national and international magazines.

These booklets have been produced with the encouragement of readers who wished to refer to a particular article which had been lost in a discarded magazine and at the suggestion of those who wanted friends, relatives and visitors in general to understand the Forest and its ways. So whether a Villager, Visitor, Tourist, or Grockle, whatever your guise, we hope these snippets will help you to understand what is so very special about this wonderful place.

FROM A NEW FOREST INCLOSURE

Following the success of the first two collections of articles written, originally, for the Burley Village magazine, 'From a New Forest Inclosure Book Three' is a compilation of the articles published in 2008 and 2009 which have been enhanced by the authors' own coloured photographs.

Within these pages you will find amusing tales from the Royal Oak; discover crazy ducks, New Forest deer and the great squirrel hunt; learn about curious collective nouns, the butcher bird and Forest bottoms!

Ian Thew

January

It's frightening to think that I have just entitled this piece as 'January 2008'. Where has 2007 gone? Well it's gone along with all the other years that preceded it – into the past; never to be re-lived again apart from, that is, in our memories. This time of the year makes us all sit up and think and, apparently, many people make major life-changing decisions in the month of January; like a change of career; a move to a new location or perhaps even a divorce! As for me? I realise that as we get older it becomes important to devote more time to the important things in life and, every New Year, I vow to do just that. So why then am I spending so much time clearing up leaves? Oh yes, they've all come down now and it seems that just about every single leaf, that once made the Inclosure so beautiful, has ended up as a sodden, brown mass, within my curtilage! I suppose that's the price I have to pay for living in such a privileged spot and, of course, it's all down, once again, to 'That Time of Year'.

But dead, soggy leaves are not all that the Forest has recently bestowed upon me – I've got mice. Not little mice, you understand, but huge mice with size ten boots and, not only that, they're mice whose nocturnal habits are upsetting my sleep pattern. It seems that they wake up or return from the mouse equivalent of the pub (probably 'The Cat & Fiddle') at about 01.30 when they proceed to mingle and have a general chat which is noisy enough to rouse me from my beauty sleep but nothing like the cacophony that follows. After about ten minutes of 'catch-up' they begin to really roister and I'm not sure if they're playing games or doing physical jerks and quite frankly I don't care; the noise is quite amazing and I lie in bed and try to imagine just what they are up to. That one, over there near the wardrobe, is clearly demonstrating how high it can spring from a ceiling joist before coming down in its clod-hoppers with a resounding thud onto the plasterboard. The one above my head is definitely 'walking the water pipe' - the tinkle of tiny feet reverberating through the copper tube is a dead give-away. And, as for those two- or is it three? – could even be four, I'm sure they're holding a steeple chase over the joists and a course that extends from one end of the attic to the other!! I vow that in the morning I'll open the hatch and set some traps but, when morning comes, it's all quiet and I kid myself that they've gone on to pastures greener and then, at 01.30 the next morning when, once again, they start to gather, I curse myself for being so complacent.

But, seriously, it's only down to 'That Time of Year' again; the weather is colder and, like the rest of us, they've moved in to keep warm. Recently, I've had several calls from worried ladies (no, not what you're thinking) who are convinced that because of the nocturnal noises that are emanating from their roof space, their house has been infiltrated by squirrels and, whilst these unwelcome, grey immigrants do, occasionally, invade our privacy, the culprits are usually mice.

Traditionally, it's thought to be the House Mouse who causes so much concern to British householders but there is evidence, which has been reported recently in the media, that the Long-Tailed Field Mouse or Wood Mouse is becoming a more and more frequent lodger. Certainly, up here in the Inclosure my unwelcome guests are the latter but, irrespective of which species you might have, make sure that you get rid of them - they can cause so much damage.

I'm not taking the Mickey!! Happy New Year

Wood mouse on bird feeder

February

Did any of you notice the sunset on Christmas day? Well, those of you who weren't sleeping off the excesses of turkey and Christmas pud may well have been, like me, walking the dogs and, as we climbed due west, up the hill, the sight was quite fantastic. Through the black skeletons of the bare winter trees the sky was illuminated by a low band of salmon pink which was topped by a clear band of powder blue, it didn't last for long and like an African sunset it just shut-down and was gone; I don't recall such a sunset before but it was a really nice Christmas present. 2007 and the winter solstice are now behind us as and we can look forward to a new year and with the days slowly drawing out we can all enjoy the subtle signs that tell us that spring is just around the corner.

Sunset over Backley Plain

In the garden the bulbs are beginning to push through into the none too warm winter sunshine and I noticed on Boxing Day that the rooks were already showing an interest in last years nests and were busily gathering in the rookery to assess any necessary, structural repairs.   The beech trees are ladened with fat buds just awaiting the signal to burst open and clothe the Forest in a new, fresh, green suit and, below Soarly Beeches in the mire, the silver birches have already developed that purple halo which is so typical of this time of the year. On the morning of New Years day I had occasion to call in at the White Buck (now there's a strange thing) and as I walked from the car to the entrance of the hotel I heard not one, but four, great spotted woodpeckers drumming on the surrounding trees. I stood for a moment to listen, surprised to hear them so early in the season, and two young men, who were having a smoke in the car park, asked me if I could tell them what was creating the noise. I explained that they were great spotted woodpeckers and that the drumming was carried out by both male and female birds as a means of proclaiming ownership of territory. They seemed to be quite excited by this revelation and hurried off to the nearest tree to try and get a sight of the noisy bird; needless to say as they approached the tree the woodpecker departed in its typical swooping flight.

There have been several sightings, in various locations on the Forest of a rather unusual and interesting winter visitor.   The great grey shrike or 'Butcher Bird' is not so 'great', in fact, it can be compared in size to a blackbird and if you are lucky enough to spot one it may be just a distant, white speck on a branch or wire.   The shrike seems to return to the same location each year where it terrorises small birds either by pursuing them in flight or by dropping on them from a vantage point.   It's very catholic in its choice of food and as well as small birds it will take insects, voles and lizards; but this bird and also its cousin the red-backed shrike have a unique habit which is quite different from all other British species.   It creates a 'larder' of food by impaling its prey on a thorn or other form of spike and will return to dine at its leisure and it's this practice together with its habit of shredding its prey that gives it the alternative name of 'Butcher Bird'.   So keep an eye out for this pied bird with a slightly hooked bill and active tail and also look for its larder – it won't be far away.

March

I was sitting in my study, up here in the Inclosure, listening to the birds and trying to identify those species which have, in the last few days, added their song to the watery tune of the robins, who sing all year round. This sudden increase in both volume and variety to the dawn chorus is a sure sign that Spring is just around the corner and I was just settling down to enjoy these delightful sounds when they were rudely shattered by a loud, metallic banging. Annoyed by this unusual interruption I poked my head through the window in an attempt to locate the source of my displeasure. There it was again – bang, bang, bang. My first thought was that an early morning driver was carrying out some adjustments to his lorry; but no, the sound was, without doubt, emanating from the direction of my paddock. Now when you live on your own in a remote location an unexplained, early morning sound, that must surely be human in origin, can raise the hairs on the back of the neck. So, with suitably raised follicles and accompanying goose bumps down the spine, I crept into the bathroom and looked through the window that looks down the garden. Bang, bang, bang it repeated; it was louder now and most definitely coming from within my property and then, suddenly, I caught a movement on the roof of the chicken shed and the culprit was revealed. A huge black crow was bashing the tin roof with repeated blows of its wicked beak; no, don't ask me why, 'cos I haven't a clue but, with murder in my heart, I banged the window and off it flew.

I was reflecting, as I settled down to work, on my murderous thoughts when it occurred to me that the collective noun for a gathering of crows might, indeed, be a 'murder' and unable to continue with my scribbling until I'd checked this out I reached for an evocatively titled book - 'The Language of Field Sports', which I knew contained a section on collective nouns. Sure enough, the venerable memory bank hadn't let me down, and the book confirmed that a *murder* of crows was correct but, alas, my eyes wandered down the page and, before I could stop myself, work went out the window and I was engrossed in some of the delightful and very apt names that our forebears had bestowed on the creatures around them. Here are some that particularly took my fancy - I hope you enjoy them too.

How about a *True Love* of turtle doves, a *paddling* of ducks, a *convocation* of eagles and a *charm* of goldfinches or, would you prefer, an *unkindness* of ravens, a *congregation* of plovers, a *building* of rooks and a *wisp* of snipe. My own personal favourite in the bird world is without doubt an *exaltation* of larks.

Not to be outdone by the birds, the animals too have been blessed with

Ferret

some unusual descriptions. Try a *shrewdness* of apes, a *glaring* of cats, a *business* of ferrets and a *skulk* of foxes, or how about a *cowardice* of curs, a *richness* of martens, a *bury* of rabbits and a *knot* of toads.

But the book went on and I discovered an *obstinacy* of buffaloes, a *pomp* of pekingese, a *strop* of razorbills, and a *slither* of sea serpents along with an *irritation* of fleas, a *scold* of magpies, a *pandemonium* of parrots and the really marvellous *helluvalot* of flies!

Mankind was not left out either and, by quoting the following, you must understand that I make no reference to any individual inhabitants of Burley! A *condescension* of actors, a *debauchery* of bachelors, an *argument* of bridge fiends and a *thrust* of gatecrashers or maybe a *corpulence* of councillors, a *vicariousness* of vicars, a *trance* of virgins and a *chatter* of M.P.s

Personally, as a snivelling writer I think that an *erudition* of editors takes some beating!

April

With the busy time for my fly fishing school just over the horizon I decided to brush-up on my own casting techniques; so off I went to a nice shallow pond or 'spalsh' (to give it its Forest name) for this pond, like several others, dries out in the summer to leave nothing more than a large, shallow depression in the grass.   Clearly, this type of pond does not support fish life but that didn't matter for all I wanted was a nice expanse of water, with its sticky, surface-tension, to practice on. To simulate a fly, I tied a short length of bright, red wool onto the end of my line and with the water lapping gently around my wellies I proceeded to work away with the rod.

It was a calm morning and the wintry sun was warming the cold earth from a deep blue sky and, to be quite honest, I was really enjoying the morning and finding the experience very therapeutic.   After about half an hour I looked up and was surprised to come face to face with a ragged old man who was mounted on an equally ragged old pony. They seemed to have emerged from nowhere and, as I watched, he kicked his worn, leather boots from ancient stirrups and allowed his cord clad legs to dangle freely. He stretched his shoulders and both pony and rider stared at me, neither of them saying a word.

"Morning "I said to break the deadlock.

He leaned forward in his creaking saddle and pointed a long and bony finger in my direction. "You won't catch nuffin in there, Nipper". He advised.

I pulled in the line and, with a grin, held up the piece of red wool for his inspection. "I know I won't. I haven't got a hook on."

He stared at me for a few more seconds and, before I could explain further, he gave a sad shake of his head, slipped his boots back into the stirrups and gently kicked the old mare. Without further ado, they moved off at a sedate walk across the grassy plain. As I stared at their retreating backs it occurred to me that tonight, I would, in all probability, be the subject of some ribald discussion around the bar of some Forest hostelry. I could just imagine the gist of the conversation – 'There he was I tell you. That fella what lives in the inclosure. Tryin' to catch a fish where there weren't nun and without a hook as well! He must be mad.'

With a shake of my own head I was about to return to my casting when my attention was caught by a rippling of the water surface near the far bank of the pond. It looked, for all the world, like a rising fish – but it couldn't be. Or could it? I placed my rod on the grass and hurried in the direction of the disturbance. No, of course it wasn't a fish but I was just as delighted by what I saw; everywhere I looked there were frogs - mating and spawning frogs that had come, from the surrounding ditches and mires, to this particular pond in order to ensure the continued survival of their species.

Since this very recent encounter I've taken a look in other areas and it seems to me that this is a bumper year for frog spawn – it's everywhere. In one, quite insignificant pond, I found a mass of spawn that was larger than any I have ever seen before and around the edges of some locations, the frogs, in their eagerness to spawn, had carelessly deposited their eggs in the depressions left by the hooves of watering ponies.

By the time you read this, a few of this plethora of eggs will have developed into wriggling tadpoles so keep an eye out for them!

Must wriggle off myself.

Casting a tag on a Forest Splash .

May

I've just heard on the radio that down in Weymouth they are filming a programme for *Eastenders*. Not Earth-shattering news, I agree, but apparently the word has gone around and thousands of people have flocked to this pretty, seaside town in the hope that they'll catch a glimpse of their silver-screen idols. This mass exodus from all over the country just goes to demonstrate how quickly and how far a rumour or fact can spread; and we humans just love a rumour – don't we? We love to talk (or rather gossip, to be more correct) and in so doing we pass information from one to another which is, more often than not, slightly distorted and, unwittingly, we create what are known as Chinese Whispers.

I'm sure that the other residents in the Forest, i.e. the animals and birds also pass whispers to each other and I'll explain why. My little oasis, up here in the inclosure, is surrounded by trees which are home to dozens of squirrels which, if I'm honest, stick to their side of the boundary for most of the year; but in the early spring things become quite different. In the middle of my property and surrounded by a considerable expanse of lawn stands a magnificent Weeping Willow tree and, just as the first buds appear, the whispers and my troubles start; and this year was no different to any other.

Two or three weeks ago, on a beautiful sunny morning, I had just lathered my face and was about to take the first swipe at my stubbled chin when I happened to glance through the window and there, hanging lazily in the trailing branches of the willow like some over-stuffed Roman Emperor, was my arch-enemy - the American invader – a grey squirrel. I was transfixed by the sight but not for long for the sharp pain as the razor incised a slice of flesh from my person brought me to my senses. I banged the window with my clenched fist and, in response, the furry little varmint casually reached out and carefully selected a bud-covered frond. With obvious relish it delicately nibbled one or two of the fattest buds and finally, to my horror, tossed the remainder of its meal onto the lawn below; and then – you won't believe this - it looked straight at my blood-dripping face and it grinned- yes, it grinned- it wasn't a nice grin either, in fact, it was more of a challenging grin and I knew then that the time had come for our annual battle to commence.

Every year I'm subjected to an unwelcome influx of these yellow-toothed pests and, despite my best efforts to repel them, the number of daily diners multiplies at an alarming rate and I have seen as many as seven of the little rodents at one sitting! But, after about three weeks, and when the first leaves appear, their visits suddenly stop and they vanish, back into the Forest, for another year. So how do they know that this tasty delicacy is awaiting their attention? I'm not paranoid, you understand, but I imagine that about mid March, some wise, old, even greyer-haired squirrel, a veteran survivor from previous conflicts, gathers a few troops around him and says something like "It's time for Thewies willow to be in bud now- lets go and wind him up! Oh, and by the way bring all your mates with you – there's plenty for everyone."

Seriously though, I am puzzled by their ability to find this tree which stands apart from all the others. Do they spot the food with their sharp little eyes or can they, perhaps, smell the new-formed buds? I don't know the answer but I am convinced that somehow they do whisper to each other.

More Forest Whisperers, next time – Chinese ones!

Weeping Willow

June

They're back! The swallows have returned to my stables. The first one was spotted on St. Georges Day but was not, apparently, the first to arrive in Burley this year. Since I first wrote about these endearing little birds, way back in August 2005, many of you very kindly contact me every year to tell me the date when your own swallows return. It has become a friendly competition and the prize this year, according to my informants, must go to the Granary Mead swallows that showed up on 4th April. I've no doubt that some of you will have recorded earlier arrivals and I'm sure that you'll let me know when! I'm not sure just how many pairs have

returned here but there are several birds flitting in and out of the half doors and would you believe that there are seven new nests under construction? I can't imagine that there are as many as seven pairs of swallows in residence so perhaps, like many other species, they build more than one nest and then select the most desirable.

Mandarin Drake

Now, let me tell you about those Chinese Whisperers that I mentioned last month. Around about mid march I was idly looking at my garden pond, which is tucked away on the southern boundary and overhung with several mature Forest beeches when, as if from nowhere, a mandarin duck dropped, with a splash, onto the water. It was a male and what a stunning sight; bedecked in multicoloured plumage it is, without doubt, one of the most eye catching birds on the Forest. A white head is topped with a bright green crown which starts at the base of its white-tipped, red bill; whilst an orange cape of feathers hang from just below the eye to rest upon a purple chest and a blue and brown back. It's most unique feature, however, is the two, huge, sail-like, orange feathers that stand upright above its tail. I was pleased to see the return of one of these pretty little ducks who are really natives of China and Japan but have successfully colonised the Forest where the ancient trees provide ample holes in which they like to nest. The very next morning I threw a generous helping of barley into the water and around the margins in order to encourage it to stay and to perhaps attract one of the rather dowdy females as well. Little did I know then just what I was getting myself into! I'd forgotten all about the whisperers!

The following evening two ducks came; the next day five; then seven and then things got entirely out of hand. Now they come in every night from all directions and what a quarrelsome and aggressive lot they are. The trouble is that whilst there can be as many as ten drakes there are never more than two females and as we all know this imbalance can lead to considerable rivalry. Round and round they pursue each other waggling their short tails and bobbing their heads in a threatening manner. Rival drakes will try to drown each other and I even saw one bird launch itself from an overhanging branch (mandarins are perching ducks) onto the back of an unsuspecting rival on the water below. Many times he tried to keep his adversary submerged but I'm pleased to say that there doesn't ever seem to be any serious outcomes to these skirmishes.

Mallard Drake

A few days ago a lone mallard drake dropped in for a feed - but not for long; the feuding mandarins signed a temporary truce and together they gave the poor mallard a right old duffing-up and he hastily departed, never to be seen again. So be careful what you do and remember the Forest whisperers are out there!

This lot are driving me quackers!

July

What a busy period of the year this is. Everything has just suddenly exploded into life; not least of which are the weeds and other house engulfing plants. Unfortunately, whilst I can deal with the weeds, the ivies and other climbers that grow on the house have, once again, taken the fancy of several species of birds and are now the location of more than a few nests, which I'm loathe to disturb with the hedge trimmer. The weather too has been quite explosive with an awful lot of unseasonably heavy rain early in June. But now, as I write this, we are heading into another day of temperatures in the mid twenties (that's around the eighties for those of you, who like me, still think in Fahrenheit).

Some of you will no doubt remember the 3rd June when it rained constantly from long before dawn until about 5 o'clock in the evening – I certainly do.

I was moping around the house bemoaning myself about the weather and trying to work up the enthusiasm to start a bit of decorating when my ramblings took me into the conservatory. I glanced unenthusiastically at the garden; but the view was distorted by the flow of huge drops of rain that raced each other, in a continual flow, down the window panes. Suddenly my interest was aroused by a blurred movement over by the pond and I immediately thought that it must be a duck; I suppose that old adage -"It's lovely weather for ducks" could well have crossed my mind. Well it was certainly true on that day for a closer look through my binoculars revealed not one, but thirteen ducks!! And, before you begin to think that the 'whisperers' had been talking again, I should tell you that the group consisted of a female mandarin with twelve, newly-fledged ducklings. Where they had come from was a mystery but, clearly, from somewhere nearby. Mandarins are tree nesting ducks and these fluffy little balls of feather, that were soon scooting round the water like clockwork toys, were only hours old and would have recently jumped, in turn, from their nest hole, probably high in a lofty old tree, to bounce unharmed on the forest floor where they would have been quickly gathered into a group by their fussing mother before being led to the water,. Following an all too brief paddle around the pond the worried duck called to her offspring and led them through the fence and back into the adjacent trees. I watched them as they disappeared and wondered just how many of the vulnerable little ducklings would survive to become fully fledged ducks. At the time I was not feeling optimistic but my hopes were raised slightly when, three days later, the group reappeared with, much to my surprise, a full compliment.

Swallow

The swallows have settled down and, despite my earlier suspicions, there is only one pair of birds in residence; which, despite attempting to build at seven new locations within the stable, have returned to the original nest which was constructed in 2006! This nest had been modified, in 2007, by an opportunist wren that had capped it off with a neat, mossy roof. Undaunted by this addition to their building work the swallows removed the offending moss and I'm pleased to report that there are now, nestling snugly in their mud cup, five, ugly, little chicks.

The great-spotted woodpeckers have also had a successful year and just now the garden is full of squabbling juveniles. I can only imagine that several nests have fledged more or less at the same time and the fights around the peanut feeders have to be seen to be believed. To my knowledge at least two of the youngsters, in their hate-fuelled haste, have flown into the conservatory glass and on both occasions, after a few dazed minutes on the ground, recovered and flew off once again to find someone else to pick a fight with.

Must go now, I'm feeling a bit peckish myself!

August

In June, I was asked to accompany the Bishop of Southampton, along with some fellow residents, for a brief walk around the bordering Forest. It proved to be an enjoyable experience and the Bishop asked some very pertinent questions about the 'ways' of the Forest – most of which we were able to answer without too much trouble. I felt very much the 'new boy', however, when he asked how long I had lived here –and my reply of "twenty-odd years" was insignificant compared to some of my fellow walkers, whose ancestors lie peacefully in the churchyard.

It occurred to me later, as I was taking some refreshment after the walk, that I have, indeed, been around long enough to see a few changes; not only changes in people but in places too. Somehow my thoughts wandered back to my early days as a Burley resident when Diane and I used to meet, on our way home after a busy day in our respective offices in Southampton, at the Royal Oak at Bank.

The 'Oak', as it was known to the regulars, was, at that time, probably one of the last bastions of a true, New Forest pub and we felt privileged to be able to join the 'locals' in the ancient, back room with its time-worn, wooden bar and its lovely old settles that had been polished to a natural sheen by generations of Forest backsides. But it was fast running out of time; the Ladies and the Gents were both outside in the garden (which presented a challenge on a cold and frosty night); cigarette and gaming machines had yet to be introduced but a well kept dartboard with its hole-pocked, oak-planked pitch and a couple of cribbage boards and a dog-eared pack of cards, together with good-humoured conversation, provided all the necessary entertainment. This worn but cosy bar was claimed by the locals as their own and woe-betide any stranger who dared to enter its hallowed portals without an invitation. Whenever possible, visitors were relegated to the tiny, front snug where they were served through a hatch in the wall from the public bar. With just a couple of bare tables and chairs, an odd stool and one or two faded photos of the surrounding Forest it didn't offer much; but I recall that a small, stuffed badger occupied the mantelpiece and, above it, mounted on the chimney breast was a moth-eaten, fox mask that stared, glassy-eyed, at the opposite wall.

Now, on the whole, Foresters are a kindly bunch, but some are renowned for their wicked sense of humour; and I remember that on one occasion a couple of strangers entered the snug and, having managed, with some effort, to secure a drink from the hole in the wall they wandered aimlessly around the small room, occasionally sipping from their glasses and scrutinising, in turn, each picture with feigned interest, as only complete new comers to a pub can.

The woman came upon the fireplace and studied the snarling badger; she then looked up and spent some time examining the unblinking fox on the chimney breast. She turned her blue-rinsed coiffure to the only other occupant of the room, who was perched on the bar stool with his long, crooked fingers wrapped around his pint of bitter, and whose presence she had failed to acknowledge beforehand.

"I say my man," she demanded in a shrill voice, pointing at the badger. "is that a fox?"

The old Forester turned his head in her direction and fixed her with his piercing blue eyes. He examined her for a moment and then followed her finger towards the badger; he glanced back through the hatch to check that his colleagues had heard the question.

"No Missus," he replied as he straightened his back. "That's a badger, that is - but that'n up there's a fox." He indicated the fox mask with a bony finger "And, before you ask," he continued with a grin, "he were goin' at one hell of a lick when he cum through that wall."

Must go now before I make a 'Charlie' of myself!

September

I counted six swallows over the stable yard this morning so I reckon they've got to be the two adult birds that arrived earlier in the season together with four of the five fledglings from their first brood which were hatched, if you remember, in the oldest of the nests. As I watched these aerial acrobats I noticed that several birds were flitting in and out of the end stable and, as curiosity got the better of me, off I went to investigate. I was surprised and delighted to discover that one of the nests, which were partially constructed earlier, had been completed and, judging by the mess on the floor below, was occupied. But occupied by whom? A second pair of breeding birds, perhaps or were they the original pair that had simply chosen a new nest site for their second brood? I had no idea and nor did I feel the need to dwell on it. These delightful birds, because of their decline over recent years, are on the Amber List of Birds of Conservation Concern; so I'm just pleased that their numbers are multiplying, if only in a miniscule way, here in this New Forest Inclosure.

Whilst we are on the subject of declining species, where are all the butterflies this year? I can see, through my study window, a Buddleia which is covered in a mass of the long purple flowers which butterflies find so irresistible that this shrub is commonly known as the butterfly bush. By rights, it should be haloed in a mass of feeding butterflies but, apart from the odd cabbage white and a lone brimstone, there has been little or no interest in it since the flowers began to open. I happened to mention my concern to a friend, who has forgotten more about butterflies than I'll ever know, and he confirmed that the numbers of both tortoiseshell and peacock butterflies seemed to be fewer this year. He went on to explain a possible, grisly reason for their apparent decline. It seems that the caterpillars, particularly those of the small tortoiseshell, whilst feeding on the leaves of nettles, unwittingly devour the eggs of a small parasitic fly, (Sturmia Bella), which was unknown in the UK before 1999 and whose invasion is attributed to either climatic change or the introduction of infected caterpillars from Europe. These ingested eggs lie dormant until they hatch, just as their hapless hosts reach the cocoon stage of their life cycle. They develop from within thus killing the developing butterflies and then, like something from the film *Alien*, the little flies burst forth from the cocoon. Apparently, those in 'the know' are desperately searching for a solution to this unwelcome phenomena but time may be running out. It has been estimated that, over recent years, the numbers of small tortoiseshells, alone, have declined by 80%!

Now after that somber tale let me cheer you with another true story from the old Royal Oak. It was getting late on a particular Autumnal evening and, as the daylight was succumbing to the enveloping darkness, a small

Red Deer

mini-bus, containing a group of visitors from nearby Southampton, pulled onto the gravelled car park. Eventually the door to the snug opened and they filed in led by a woman of considerable stature; clearly a leader, she marched purposefully toward the waiting landlord.

"There's a herd of deer in the road." She barked, at the same time pointing in the general direction from whence she had come.

The landlord, a man not often lost for words, looked puzzled by this unusual form of greeting and, despite giving some serious consideration to a suitable response, could only say "Well this is the New Forest – they do live here, you know."

Clearly the harridan was not best pleased with his response. She hoisted her ample bust onto the bar and leaned forward so that her face was inches from his. "I'm aware of that you silly man - but isn't somebody going to shut them in for the night?!

Silly old dear!

October

It's raining – well pouring actually and I'm beginning to wonder when it's going to stop. We're already well into September and the weather to date can hardly be described as seasonal. Last month had been decreed, by those in the know, as the wettest August on record and, if September continues as it started, it could be a strong contender for a similar accolade. At this time of the year, when working in my study, I should be listening, through open widows, to the sounds of walkers, riders and cyclists as they enjoy the delights of this part of our beautiful New Forest - but not today; the rain is hammering on closed windows and the only other sound is from the dogs who, on this most dismal of days, have lost interest and lie snoring vociferously beneath my desk. I can't remember when it seemed so deserted up here but I can liken it to that terrible period back in 2001 when the Forest was closed to visitors because of the nearby outbreak of Foot and Mouth; the only movement at that time, apart from the odd Forestry Commission vehicle, was the daily visit from the postman – and even he hasn't been today!

Well at least it's warm and it is, so they say, "An ill wind that blows nobody any good" and, from a purely personal point of view, the weather has been perfect for me to indulge in one of my favourite, but often unpredictable, pastimes – wild fungi foraging. All over the Forest and in the most unexpected and sometimes never-before-seen places wild fungi are popping-up in great profusion. What a delight it is to see great drifts of the suede-like Hedgehog mushrooms, often interspersed with the egg-yolk yellow eyes of the delicate Chanterelles, as they march boldly across the leaf litter on the Forest floor. On mossy banks beneath the beech trees the black, velvety trumpets of the Horn of Plenty stand row upon row like so many open mouths. Their sombre appearance and their alternative name of Trompettes des Morts dissuade the less courageous of gatherers from taking advantage of such a rare find and, as I gather my fill, I sometimes feel sad for these poor individuals (but not often), who will never experience the delicate flavour of these enigmatic fungi that are, on occasion, used by unscrupulous chefs as an alternative to the more expensive truffles. I don't know if, by the time you read this, there will be a fungi crop to gather but if you do forage please remember to pick only those species that you can identify with certainty as edible and please,

please, pick enough for your own consumption only and leave plenty behind to ensure a taster for years to come.

Parasol Mushroom

As I watch the relentless rain I remember a day many years ago when it was so hot that for mutual comfort the ponies stood nose to tail outside the Royal Oak. One clever pony stood with its head through an open window as if waiting to be served but, in reality, was seeking some respite from the ever-persistent flies. The man from the council had dropped in for an unexpected inspection of the premises - but no one seemed bothered. He went out the back to inspect the loos and soon returned with a triumphant smirk. He walked directly to the laconic landlord who was propping-up the bar and slapped his briefcase onto the polished surface.

"There's a huge spider in a dirty web in the corner of the gents' toilet." He spread his hands to demonstrate the size of this offensive find.

The landlord shifted position slightly and gazed slowly around the bar. "See any flies in here?" he asked.

The Health Inspector, clearly perturbed and frustrated by this unexpected response, looked around the room. "Well, now that you mention it – no, I don't."

"Well then, Mister - spider's doin' his job then – idn't he?" A broad grin crept across the landlords face and more than one local chuckled into his beer.

Must go now and check the Web

November

It's mid October and after one of the wettest summers in memory we have, for the past few days, been basking in summer-like sunshine. There is no doubt, however, that things are on the change. The south of England awoke this morning to find that it was shrouded in a heavy fog and, as I walked the dogs through the Douglas firs, the tops of these lofty trees faded into a hidden, misty world. The junction of the gravel tracks, which I knew was surely there, not three hundred yards away, was, too, lost in this magic miasma. In the distance a mournfully, bellowing cow called continuously for its calf - a rather spine-tingling addition to this ethereal dawn. I looked back in the direction of the cottage and could see only the vague outline of the building; we were, for a little while anyway, in a strange and eerie world.

Down by the brook the dogs stopped abruptly and looked at me with that 'there's something out there Guvnor' look. I clicked my fingers and they came close as we proceeded quietly towards the stream. My eyes narrowed as they tried to locate the source of their concern and at the same time the hairs on the back of the Labrador became erect and a low growl rumbled from his barrel-like chest. This, together with the sound of the mournful cow had a similar effect on the hairs on the back of my neck and we waited, hardly daring to breathe, as together we focussed on a slowly emerging outline on the track ahead. It was a fallow buck who, without a care in the world, was walking, his magnificent head held high, down the middle of the road. He became suddenly aware of our presence and, after a brief scrutiny, he disappeared into the fog as quietly as only a deer can.

With some relief we continued our walk, making a wide sweep before turning towards home from a westerly direction. Slowly, at first, and then with a suddenness that was surprising, the sun eventually burnt its way through, dispersing the fog and presenting a whole new world. In the warming sunshine, the dew glistening on a million cobwebs transformed every single fuzz bush into a unique delight; whilst the clear, cloudless sky above was embroidered by enumerable jets streams – some bold and firm whilst others, less recent, faded into obscurity. The early-morning chill quickly became a memory and sun-warmed squirrels were soon scampering across the Forest floor as they busied themselves with their harvest festival, and the discarded, prickly, sweet chestnut husks which adorned almost every tree stump gave testament to their good fortune.

It wasn't long before I too began to feel the heat and regretted that I had been so generous with my outer garments, when I had set-out this morning; so it was with some relief, for both the dogs and myself, when , on reaching home, we were able to take some liquid refreshment.

Fallow Buck

Before I settled down to my key-board, at the end of an unseasonably scorching day, I decided to give the dogs a last turn around the inclosure and what a difference this was when compared to our early-morning walk. The evening sun burnished the now golden leaves on the silver birches and I was somewhat surprised to note that the sweet chestnut branches were almost bare. Alongside the track an ominous looking panther cap mushroom poked its scaly head through the newly fallen leaves whilst overhead, and beneath the canopy of yellowing beech leaves, a few tiny, pipistrelle bats, hawked for pre-hibernation flies. The sweet, heady smell of haylage was in the air and as I turned towards the lazy curl of wood smoke that drifted from my chimney I realised that autumn was here again.

December

The half-term holiday was blessed with warm and sunny days and the Forest was alive with visitors who had come to enjoy the last break before Christmas. I rested on a seat for a while and watched them go by: walkers, runners, horse riders, carriage drivers and of course cyclists – cyclists by the hundred and of every shape and age. I sat there for longer then I should have and pondered over the different types that had passed me by.

The elite group of cyclist must surely be the Racers; clad in body-hugging, Forest-blending, purple or yellow, Lycra which accentuates every curve, bump and protrusion beneath, and bedecked with strange, rearward pointing helmets, these paragons of the cycling world fly along the tracks. Usually male (all though I have seen some nice looking female versions) they are mounted on sleek, light-weight machines, no doubt created from space-age technology and, with heads down over their drooping handle bars and bums pointing skyward, they are oblivious to all that's around them. The only warning of their breakneck approach might be the slight hiss of ridiculously narrow tyres as they skim across the gravel, but be sure to jump out of their way for they see nothing and say nothing; they are totally absorbed in their mission which seems to be the attainment of the fastest possible time through the most stunning of English environments! Perhaps the A31 would be more suited to their needs.

Mountain-bikers on the other hand are a much tougher bunch; trainers, shorts and a thin t-shirt are their preferred outfits. Their machines too, are far more robust and practical; built from galvanised scaffold tube and mounted on Massey-Ferguson tyres they are indestructible and, clearly, designed to go where no man has ventured before. Whilst the Racers make a mockery of the Inclosure speed limits the Mountain-bikers scorn the 'keep to the gravel track' rule and scoff at the potential £500.00 fine for defying it. The object of their exercise, it seems, is to locate and then plunge themselves and their machines into any bog that's capable of devouring a 'Coach and Four'; and if they're fortunate enough to survive the ordeal they'll emerge from the other side covered in mud and mire but, more importantly, deliriously happy.

Bike-hirers are another, ever-growing, group of enthusiasts. A typical family might be observed as they leave the village in single file, hell-bent on enjoying their first cycle ride for years. Typically Mum will be in the lead with two or three wobbly kids between her and Dad, who is bringing up the rear with the baby in a trailer. What a happy bunch they are, laughing and shouting cheerfully to each other, as they set off for a day in the Forest; but little do they know just what the fickle hand of fate could have in store for them.

Forest bog

They quickly discover that loose gravel is harder to pedal over than smooth tarmac and aching muscles begin to take the shine of the venture. One of the children, who is nursing a cut hand and a grazed knee, is now aware that gravel can also be very unforgiving if you fall of your bike and make contact with at fifteen miles per hour. Mum has dismounted and is now pushing her cycle up a steep incline, with one hand, and dragging her bawling offspring's' bike, with its buckled wheel, in the other. Meanwhile, Dad, who knows by now that he is not as fit as he thought he was and encumbered by the added weight of his youngest in the trailer, is so far behind that he is out of sight. But having paid for the hire he is determined that, at all costs, his family will enjoy their day out – or perhaps they'll turn back and go to the pub after all - he's just noticed that his rear tyre has a puncture!

Have a very happy Christmas and if you get a bike – don't blame me!

January

Many of you seemed to enjoy last months, light-hearted spoof on cyclists but, because of editorial restrictions on lineage which, quite rightly, prevent me from rambling on ad nauseum, I didn't have the space to discuss a further category of cyclists that, perhaps, should've been mentioned. This group are what I call the 'Dog Draggers'. Fortunately they are not that common but I suspect that we've all spotted one or two of this species, especially since the advent of the New Forest National Park! I cannot believe that anyone can be so thoughtless that they could tie poor old Fido to their bicycles in order to exercise him, so I'll assume that they just don't know any better! Clearly, these people don't realise that a dog likes to set its own pace, to be able to wander around to sniff and savour each tantalisingly new smell; but, more importantly, it needs to be able to slow down or stop when its tired; it needs to be able to drink when its thirsty and it needs to be able to answer the call of nature when necessary - none of which it can do when being dragged behind an inconsiderate owner. During the summer I encountered two incidents of dogs that had collapsed through heat and exhaustion simply because their unthinking owners had taken them for a cycle-drag around the Inclosure. On each occasion the animals were extremely distressed and I wouldn't want to witness similar situations again.

Now, on a more cheerful note, how about starting the New Year by acquiring another skill?   Here's something that I learned many years ago whilst working in the construction industry; a time so far back that we didn't have any new-fangled, electronic equipment to call upon when we wanted to locate buried cables, water pipes and drains. It's a form of dowsing and, before you pick–up the phone to tell me that this is the realm of wizened old men bearing flimsy willow wands, who've been blessed with a magical gift that's been passed-down through generations of forebears, let me tell you that I believe that we can all do this. The only bits of equipment you need are the dowsing rods and these can be made from any stiff wire such as a wire coat-hanger, fence straining wire, welding rods, etc. Take two pieces of wire about 600mm long (that's 2'0" to those of us who still work in old money!) and put a right-angled bend in each length, about 150mm (6") from one end; with a bit of luck you should now have two L-shaped lengths of wire. The next step is to test them out, so go outside and find something obvious like a drain run between two manholes. Stand to one side of the line of the drain and with the shortest leg of a rod gripped loosely in each hand and with the longer leg pointing forward (like someone pointing a pistol), walk slowly towards the drain, keeping the hands at chest height and about 300mm (12") apart. With a bit of luck and some practice, as you pass over the buried drain, the rods will, magically, swing towards each other and cross-over in front of your very eyes.

Go on, try it, it really is quite amazing and can be very useful, but don't ask me to explain how it works; all I know is that over the years I have located the line of buried pipes, cables, water services and even dried and empty earthenware land-drains. Just remember that this only seems to work if you actually cross over the line of whatever it is that you're trying to locate; in other words, if you walk your rods along the length of the water service or drain then they won't respond. Have fun!

Must go now before you all dowse-off!

Have a prosperous New Year.

February

The pleasant but cold weather over the Christmas holiday encouraged an unprecedented number of visitors into the Inclosure and with them they brought their dogs; dogs of every shape and description- happy dogs, miserable dogs, obedient dogs and totally-out-of-control dogs.

Out-of-control dogs come in various forms but can usually be identified by their remoteness from their owner. In fact some visitors to our Forest don't see their beloved Fido from the minute he's released from the car until the moment he returns, which, in most cases, will be long after they've regained the sanctuary of their vehicle. When questioned about their four legged friend, who's chasing ponies in the distance, they usually deny all ownership; only to be embarrassed when Rover, with untypical faithfulness, returns to sit obediently at their side and with heaving chest and lolling tongue, gazes adoringly into their eyes. Some visitors, however, do make an effort to control their wayward pets and the extending dog lead has become an indispensable part of their armoury. These owners can be identified, even without their dog, by their ground-dragging, gibbon-like arms, which have been developed over a period of time by attempting to restrain their beloved hound as it's pulled them along, with the strength of a team of huskies, at the end of a forty foot length of nylon cord. There is one major drawback with these lengthy restraints, especially in a forest full of trees – Yes, you've guessed it. Dogs don't walk in straight lines – do they? They like to wander around and sniff about. Their ultra-sensitive noses might take them right around one tree and then back to another to check on a tantalising smell- then across to and around a nearby oak - and hey ! There goes a squirrel. So it's off again and round and round a hefty beech bole and before you know it you've got a round turn and two half-hitches followed by an assortment of unnamed knots that would require the assistance of most of the Burley scouts to unravel!

In contrast, working breeds are usually (but not always) under control and obedient to their masters' every whim. These dogs have an inbred desire to work for their owners – it's in their blood to please and these paragons of the doggie world 'clock-on' to their job as soon as their paws cross a cattle grid.   Haughty Labradors, probably the elite of this group, especially the black ones, trot sedately at heel treating everything around with disdain unless, of course, it's a pheasant! Elegant pointers range a little further in front of their human companions, occasionally stopping suddenly to point, with raised paw and rigid tail, at some tantalising smell. And then there are the spaniels; fearless and tireless they hunt through the undergrowth with utter abandon – the more scratches on their muzzles and the more burrs in their coats when they return to their car – then the happier they will be. Terriers come in all shapes and sizes but you might not see much of these for they are inclined to live up to their name by heading straight for the nearest rabbit bury, fox earth or badger set from whence, for the next few hours, their frantic owners will be frustrated by their constant, muffled yapping from deep within the bowels of the earths. No amount of coaxing or cajoling will encourage one of these intrepid fighters to emerge. Then, suddenly, without any explanation and usually as the light is just fading, out it will pop; infested with fleas, covered from head to paws in stinking soil, its muzzle scratched and bleeding, but deliriously happy!

We mustn't leave out the miserable dogs. Usually poodles, Yorkies and similar lap dogs these 'Townies' have been lured away from the central heating and dressed in neat little coats to be dragged reluctantly along the track. They're clearly unhappy in this alien environment; see how they place delicate pads on the rough gravel– just watch how they step carefully around the puddles, how they turn their noses up at the unfamiliar smells and how they frequently stop and turn to look from whence they've come. Our beautiful Forest is not for these puny canines, their only thought is to get back to their warm and cosy beds.

And in this weather, that's not a bad idea!

March

It's early February and the heaviest snowfall for nineteen years has brought much of the country to a grinding halt. This adds insult to injury for we've already been subjected to some pretty severe weather, this year – I don't know what's happened to global warming but it doesn't seem to be an issue as I sit here, at my desk, and watch the snow falling beyond the window.

Snow on Woolfield Hill

The birds in the garden have been emboldened by this harsh weather and take little or no evasive action when approached. I'm sure that it must take an awful lot of searching to find enough food with which to generate the energy for a short flight and, consequently, they are only taking to the wing if absolutely necessary. Male blackbirds and robins that, a few days ago, were squabbling and sparring with each other, (no doubt over the charms of some likely females), have signed a truce and take little or no notice of each other as they forage in the snow-free, leaf litter under the garden shrubs. Survival is their only concern during these hard times and I've noticed that one or two enterprising birds have taken to roosting in the workshop and the stables - and good luck to them!

Recently, on one very cold day, I noticed that a heron had come to pay a visit to my little pond. Now, under normal circumstances, a visit from one of these grey marauders would normally send me into a rage, for they have feasted on my fish on more than one occasion and I am determined that they won't 'dine-out' on me again. On this occasion, however, I had no need to be concerned for the well-being of the inhabitants of the pond; it was sealed by a crust of ice that was so thick, that only a few hours earlier, it had taken my full weight without a creak or a crack of complaint.

I took some time to watch the bird. It was a pitiful sight; hunched against the bitter cold on the ice-rimed bank, it's long, snakelike neck tucked well-in and out of sight and the wicked, spear of a beak hanging down, over its breast, like a useless appendage. I grabbed the binoculars for a closer inspection; eyes that would normally be alert to the slightest movement were tightly closed and when I tapped the window they failed to respond. It reminded me of a sad, old, man who has given up on life and is just waiting for his time to come. For once, I felt some compassion for this stealer of fish.

It was some time later when I looked out again and was surprised to see that the bird had roused itself and was stalking, as only a heron can, with barely perceptible movements, across the icy pond. As I watched, it spotted some movement in the water below and froze into a motionless statue. Without warning the vicious beak stabbed at the ice and I could almost feel the headache that it must have received from the unyielding impact. Clearly, this bird was desperately hungry but what could I do? The answer came to me in a flash. In the larder a fat, summer-caught trout was defrosting for my supper and no, I didn't give it that! But I did take off the fillets and put the unwanted head, tail and backbone on the ice-bound pond.

They were gone the next morning. Could've been the heron or it could've been a Charlie - who knows?

Whoever it was had a bone to pick with me!

April

There are three ponies, in particular, who haunt the part of the forest that surrounds my property – two New Forest ponies and a little, coloured Shetland who boasts one brown eye and one blue eye which makes him, as far as I'm concerned, either charming or spooky, depending on which eye he uses when looking at me. They've been around here for some time and, if I'm honest, they have never been a problem. They make an appearance, every once in a while, and spend a day or two cropping the grass beyond my fence before they disappear once again to wherever the idea takes them.

One day, not long ago, when the snow lay thick on the ground, I'd noticed that the aforementioned trio were standing in a miserable huddle and staring through the fence at the hay bales in the lean-to behind the stable. I felt a twinge of guilt every time I passed by this doleful bunch and I felt more sorry for them as the day wore on and the temperature, that had crept to just above freezing, began to fall with alarming speed. There was a part-used bale of hay on the top of the stack and before I could stop myself I had opened the side gate and spread it out in three little heaps. The hungry ponies fell on the offering and I was rewarded by the sound of contented munching each time I neared the gate. I felt pleased with myself and the little bit of guilt, that lurked in the back of my mind, for feeding Forest ponies, was dismissed by the thought that I didn't live near a highway and so, consequently, the ponies were in no danger.

But it had been a big mistake! I should have known better. The very next day, although the snow had now melted away, and at precisely the same time, they were back. They stood in a similar huddle and stared at the hay bales and, every time I appeared, they fixed me with pathetic faces. Each time I walked toward the side gate they followed on the other side of the fence. Up and down they walked; turning the thawing snow and the grass beneath, into a quagmire. They stamped their feet and churned the gate entrance into a boggy mess and, to add insult to injury, the ungrateful, blue-eyed, little devil began to kick the gate whilst one of her buddies pulled great clumps from my neatly clipped hedge.

I shooed them on their way but they came the next day and the next. On the fourth day I returned from a shopping trip to discover them grouped

37

around my front gates. I drove them off and they retreated back into the trees – but not for long. I began to unload my shopping and, on the second trip from car to kitchen, I was so ladened with bags that I didn't close the gate properly and - yes, you've guessed it – in they came. I heard a crunch on the gravel and turned from my task to be greeted by the tiny Shetland who framed the doorway in her quest for food. This was the last straw and, after much shouting, waving and air-bluing, I managed to evict them.

Eventually they gave up and left me in peace but not before they had wrecked my driveway, devastated the hedge and left scratch marks on the boot and bonnet of my car!

Sometimes, it just doesn't pay to do a kindness – or perhaps I should say interfere!

New Forest Pony

May

I'm not suggesting that my lovely black Labrador, Benson (yes, the brother of Hedges) is accident prone but in the relatively short time that he has been part of the Burley Mouse Hounds he's had his share of misfortunes. Two years ago he managed to impale himself on a spike of 'spiny' oak that was as thick as and as long as my middle finger. The iron-hard chunk of oak entered near the rib cage and finished up beneath his skin at the base of his tail! Fortunately, his injury was not life-threatening but it did cause him some discomfort for several weeks and the damage inflicted on my wallet by the Vets' fee caused me some severe discomfort too! More recently he damaged his eye, probably by running into a something sharp. This developed into a painful ulcer which took several weeks of treatment and more of the old folding stuff before it healed. It was a credit to the Vets skill that the dog didn't have to undergo surgery which would've meant, no doubt, another mortgage!

They say that misfortunes come in threes and Benson proved to be no exception to this rule when, last Sunday, he was run over by a bicycle-here in the Inclosure. We had all been for a good walk along the river and had just reached the main track to Bolderwood when down the hill came a jolly bunch of tourist on their hire bikes. Now most cyclists will steer around any animals that they encounter and conversely most dogs will move out of the path of an on-coming cyclist but sometimes circumstances can defy the norm. Indeed, Mum, who was in the lead, eased-up when she saw us but not so her young son who clearly was not aware of the danger and hurtled past his mother at a goodly speed. Too late he spotted the dog and clamped on his brakes. The dog meanwhile was oblivious to his imminent fate and was engaging the Mother with one of his pathetic 'I need feeding' looks. Now, when 50 kilos of speeding boy encounters 30 kilos of black dog, something has to give - and it wasn't the dog. In a shower of stones and with groaning brakes the lads' bike struck the solid dog. The bike stopped but, alas, the boy didn't; he flew over the handlebars in a graceful curve and landed in a tangle of arms and legs on the unresisting gravel. The dog, meanwhile, lay on his side beneath the bicycle and for one heart-stopping moment he didn't stir. My companion rushed to pick-up the lad and, at the same time, I lifted the bike from the somewhat startled dog. Now Benson is a real gentleman and a lesser dog might have retaliated by biting the boy who, in turn, showed his true colours by not biting the dog either! In fact the boy and the dog were both stalwarts; neither uttered a sound. The dog had a good shake to rid himself of the dust and debris that he had acquired during the accident and then wandered over to enquire into the wellbeing of the young fellow.   The lad was nursing a cut elbow and a grazed chin and clearly he was both shocked and hurt but he never said a word nor did he shed any tears.

Fortunately neither the boy nor the dog sustained any serious injuries and after washing both off in the stream we watched as the family remounted and went on their way. It was a sobering reminder to everyone that accidents can so easily happen – so do be careful out there!

It's late, so now I'm going to crash too!

Big Black Labrador

June

Did you know that, this year, the first day of spring fell on 20th March? Apparently, spring comes in-between the 19th to the 23rd of March; the exact date being dependant on the occurrence of the Vernal Equinox which is when the sun is directly above the equator and this doesn't necessarily happen on the exact same day every year. But never mind all that – what a wonderful spring we are having!

This year, violets were the first wild flowers to make an appearance in my part of the Inclosure and the grass verges alongside the Forest tracks are, even now, smothered in their delicate, blue blooms. The paddocks too have been a picture; a few weeks ago yellow celandines and primroses together with pink and white anemones crept out from the Forest edge and into the marginal grasses. They are past their best now but have been reinforced by the tall spikes of bugle; long spindly cuckoo flowers or milkmaids and a fragrant, hazy covering of bluebells. The blackthorn clump and the ancient bramley apple tree have been covered in a mass of blossom which has managed, because of the unusually calm weather, to hang on for a good length of time this year – perhaps this will mean a bumper harvest later on.

On the open Forest the air is heady with the scent of the gorse blossom which, this year, seems to be more vibrant than ever. And, in the Inclosure, the beech and ash trees are newly clothed in fresh, green leaves; the more observant will note that both species bear a profusion of well concealed flowers so, perhaps, beech mast and acorns will be an autumnal feature, once again.

But, as with all things in life, where there are 'ups' there are, usually, 'downs' and, as each new beech leaf appears, so a tiny brown husk, that once formed the outer covering of each bud, will float down from above. I first noticed these floral rejects a couple of weeks ago when I was applying a new coat of wood stain to the conservatory. I was about halfway through my task and pleased with the results, thus far, when a playful breeze decided to intervene and spoil my day. This mischievous zephyr, without warning, evicted thousands of husks from their lofty abode and carried many of them with uncanny accuracy to alight on my handiwork where they formed a close affiliation with the sticky paint. Within a few minutes my pristine conservatory looked more like a gross

41

hedgehog clinging to the side of the house. Needless to say I was devastated and my futile efforts to evict them made matters worse but I am pleased to say that the next day, when the stain had cured, the 'prickles' were easily removed with a stiff brush.

Gorse or Fuzz in bloom

And then, of course there are the mandarin ducks. Yes, they've returned to the pond again and they seem to be even more aggressive than before. The drakes outnumber the ducks and so infighting is the norm but woe betide any other bird species that dares to invade their space. Clearly, before they left their native China to invade this fair land of ours, all had been carefully instructed in the mysteries of martial arts. They are fearless fighters and, only last evening, I watched as a foolish crow crossed their boundary; without hesitation or warning a black-belted Chinaman launched an unprecedented attack on this heavily-armed intruder and, in a blur of feathers and paddles, he gave the corvid what I believe is referred to as a 'good duffing-up'.

So, if a mandarin comes near – duck!

July

Just as I was about to remortgage the house in order to buy yet another, very expensive, sack of bird food, my garden visitors disappeared. Feeding stations, which so recently had been smothered in squabbling tits and finches, were all but deserted. No longer was it necessary to refill them on a daily basis for, apart from an occasional woodpecker or nuthatch, nothing came to feed. The wood mice, however, had a whale of a time, taking advantage of the lull in birds they clambered up to the wire cages where they hung like dare-devil, circus performers as they gorged themselves on the tasty peanuts and seeds. It was that time of year again. Procreation had taken precedence over everything else and the birds were, generally, busily feeding their nestlings; and not on peanuts or sunflower seeds but on tasty, nutritious morsels gleaned from the Forest. High in the broadleaved trees, birds of many species were gathering food for their hungry broods. Time after time I watched as they flew off with beaks full of wriggling caterpillars, flies, lacewings and many other unidentifiable insects, returning within seconds to continue their never-ending task. On the lawn and in the paddocks an ever-changing stream of blackbirds and their close relations the song thrushes hopped about, heads cocked to one side, listening for the movement of insects and earthworms as they hunted for food to fill the gaping maws of their insatiable broods. Without doubt, there was a plethora of nests in and around the garden and I was soon to discover some that had been constructed under my very nose without my knowledge.

Whilst brewing my early morning tea I noticed that in the climbing hydrangea, immediately adjacent to the kitchen window, a pair of robins had taken up residence. I must have been clearly visible through the glass but they took no notice of me, as, in turn, they carried load after load of food to their nest. Not long after this discovery I was surprised, whilst shaving, by another beak-ladened, robin that suddenly appeared on the bathroom window-sill. It was, clearly, unconcerned by the lathered face that stared at it through the leaded lights. It tipped its head slightly in my direction and regarded me with its bright little eye and, without a care, it hopped into the ivy and, having made the delivery to its secret nest, it flew off once again to continue the cycle.

My inferior offerings have remained untouched for a week or two; but now, just as if someone has thrown a switch, the birds are back with a vengeance; and they're not on their own – they've brought the kids with them and what a motley crew they are! There are young tits everywhere; some very wobbly and unsure of their wings; many with tufts of down on their crowns giving the impression that they've just got out of bed, which in fact, I suppose, they have; and some, which occasionally, disturb my crossword as they bump into the conservatory windows.

Great spotted woodpecker feeding on peanuts

Not least of all are the great-spotted woodpeckers which frequently encourage an offspring onto the post that supports the bird table. Here the red-capped, gormless-looking juveniles cling, whilst mum or dad runs up the post to snaffle a peanut from the wire cage above, then back down again to hammer the food into a fissure in the timber, whereupon they proceed to feed the clamouring youngster with nutty fragments. But, no sooner has the adult bird turned its back and shinned up the post for another nut, the not-so-gormless pecker will usually proceed to delve into the crack for any remaining morsels!

Must go before someone takes a peck at me!

August

I went to the supermarket this morning; it's not one of my favorite pastimes but the larder was looking pretty bare so I was forced to grit my teeth and replenish the shelves and, after dodging my way around the crowded aisles for a good half hour, my disposition could not be described as friendly! However, the cheery smile and pleasant "good morning" from the lady at the till, when I pushed my sagging trolley up to the checkout, gave my spirits a lift and I was thankful that my onerous task was nearly completed. Then she went and spoiled my morning by asking "Would you like some bags, today"?

Now, I have to tell you that I was not in the mood to answer such an inane question but, in deference to her pleasant manner, I suppressed the 'Victor Meldrew' reply that hovered on my lips and simply nodded my head at my pile of purchases and gave her what I hoped was a pleading smile. Clearly, the clever woman had been here before and she knew that, today, I was not to be trifled with.

"Of course you do." She said as she proceeded to unravel a few plastic carriers for me.

Her question, of course, was compulsory and is repeated for every customer, for we are being discouraged from using their hitherto free, plastic carriers because of an 'environmental issue'. Instead, we are encouraged to purchase 'bags for life' or biodegradable bags that have been woven from natural fibres and fabrics and, I suppose, before long, the supermarket carrier will become a thing of the past.

Now, I can only speak for myself, but life without a few plastic bags hanging on the back of the larder door, would not be the same. A day does not go by without finding a use for one or two of them. Indeed, as I write, there's one lining the waste-paper bin, here in my study; if I'm successful after a visit to the fishery, I use one to carry my catch home and then I re-use it to wrap-up the entrails before disposal; and they're frequently utilised by grateful family and friends to carry away the surplus vegetables from my garden. In fact, the supermarket carrier must have hundreds of uses.

Later, when I pulled-up outside the house I was trying to think of more ways that could be employed to re-cycle plastic bags. I happened to glance down the track and there, in the sun-dappled shadows, I saw a man approaching and, believe it or not, dangling from his hand was a white, supermarket carrier. I knew, before I asked, just what it contained.

"Morning" I said, "Found a few early mushrooms?"

"Oh, just a few Chanterelle." He replied. "Found 'em over there, down the side of your house" His ancient and floppy hat wobbled precariously as he nodded in that general direction before he shuffled on his way.

But that's not all! An hour or so later, as I was driving along Mill Lane, I spotted two females in the distance. Not so unusual, you might think, but there they were, one each side of the road, walking slowly along the verges, and, you might find this difficult to believe, but they too had plastic

Vegetables are frequently given away in carrier bags

carriers! You will forgive me for immediately thinking that they were also collecting mushrooms but, as I drove slowly past them, all was revealed– they were not picking fungi - they were picking litter! Bless 'em.

So, there you are, two more enterprising uses for re-cycled carriers – can we live without them? I doubt it.

Must go now before I get carried away too!

September

Those of you who have nothing better to do than read my monthly ramblings may well recall that I have, on occasion, mentioned Gods' Gate, which is situated in the boundary fence of North Oakley Inclosure. You may also remember me telling you that it gets this name from the legend 'ALL THIS BEAUTY IS OF GOD' that, many years ago, had been carved into a small piece of wood and fixed to the underside of the top rail of the small, wicket gate that hangs alongside the larger, vehicular gate.

Gods' Gate is a beautiful spot and I often think about the author of the legend. Indeed, I have made numerous enquiries, on this subject, among the older members of the community, but the identity of the creator of the words remains a mystery. But go yourself and lean on the gate (you'll have to imagine that the tiny Lorries crawling along the distant A31are not there) and you'll look over a view that is hard to match in this Forest of ours. The graveled track known as Sandy Ridge snakes across open Forest towards the ancient hulk of Bratley Wood. To the right of this track open heath land drops gently away in the direction of Bratley Water; whilst, to the left, the heather-clad ground tumbles steeply into Backley Bottom, Soldiers' Bog and Stinking Edge Wood. Not really names for a beauty spot but go and see for yourself you won't be disappointed. Now turn around. Rest your back on the gate and look up into the magnificent Douglas Firs, that are said to be direct descendants of the original plants imported by Douglas himself and are among the tallest of trees in the Forest, and, like me, you might just begin to appreciate how, long ago, someone - perhaps a woodman or keeper- was sufficiently moved to take a piece of wood and carve into it

'ALL THIS BEAUTY IS OF GOD'.

Now, I have to tell you that if you do go there you'll still find the old wicket hanging on its venerable hinges which were, no doubt, hand-forged with pride by a local blacksmith who must be long-since gone; and, if you look carefully, you'll still be able to find the small length of timber which was carefully fixed, all those years ago, under the top rail of the gate. But no matter how hard you look you will not be able to read those simple words that were written with such feeling; for some mindless individual, for whatever reason, has seen fit to take a knife and obliterate the carving!

It saddens me to think that all the painstaking and heartfelt work by the originator should be destroyed for no apparent reason other than shear vandalism and, as one of our keepers pointed out when I mentioned

Replaced legend on Gods Gate

it to him, the origin of the name Gods' Gate will, like so many other place names, be lost in the passing of time. So I think it should be replaced and that's just what I'm going to do!

Now I've got that of my chest, what about the butterflies? In August 2008 I was bemoaning the fact that there was a dearth of butterflies on my Buddleia flowers. I'm pleased to say that this is not the case, this year – the blooms are heaving with a plethora of multi-hued insects. On one sunny day (yes, we did have at least one sunny day) this week I counted ten species of butterflies in one sitting.

Good Old Mother Nature - she usually manages to balance her books.

Must flutter off myself

October

Take a walk up Castle Hill Lane and before long you will come to Burley Beacon and, if you happen to go up there after dark, don't be surprised if the hairs on the back of your neck begin to prickle; for this can be an eerie place. It's reputed to be the one-time home of the Burley Dragon; a fearsome beast that terrorised the residents of nearby Bisterne when it flew down, on a regular basis, to demand a pail of milk upon threat of damage to 'man and cattle' if it wasn't forthcoming! The good people of Bisterne got fed-up with this and enlisted a 'knight in shining armour' well actually he was, apparently, a knight who coated himself in birdlime and broken glass. His name was Sir Moris Berkley and he engaged the dragon in a fierce battle in which his two dogs were slain and he was mortally wounded, but not before he had killed the dragon. Since that time and thanks to Sir Moris the residents of Castle Hill have been able to sleep easily in their beds – or have they?

Close by to Burley Beacon live a very nice family. They have toiled and planted and created a beautiful garden where they are wont to sit and admire the stunning view over Cranes Moor and the distant Dorset hills. Last year they had a spot of bother with some tiresome moles that had taken up residence under their newly sown grass. I was enlisted to solve the problem; and solve it I did without too much fuss. Peace and tranquillity were restored and continued for months until, quite recently, I received a further summons from the man of the house to rid their home of yet another mole – "It's a big one" he said.

Now I'm used to people ringing up and bemoaning the fact that their gardens are infested with hundreds of moles, rabbits or deer when, in truth, it doesn't take many of either to create havoc, thus giving the impression of an invasion. So I took his comment with a pinch of salt – what a mistake that was! I poodled up to the property and sauntered light-heartedly down the garden. I turned the corner of the house and there, huddled together like ancient pyramids, were four of the biggest molehills I've seen. The lady of the house appeared "We've called it the Mutant" she said. I assured her that it was just a mole and that I would catch it in a trice.

49

Now there have been times in my life when I wished I had simply kept quiet - and this was one of them. I set some traps into the tunnels and returned the next day. I was surprised to find that two of the traps had been thrown up onto the lawn and annoyed by the presence of two more enormous heaps of soil, each large enough to solve the traffic calming problems in the village, that my subterranean foe had pushed-up from below. I set more traps and returned on the following morning; yet another trap had been tossed out and more heaps had appeared. I realised then that I was dealing with something beyond the norm and laid even more traps before I left.

The situation worsened as day after day I returned to find more and more devastation. I became obsessed with this Mutant, I would lay awake at night and worry, I dreaded each visit and having to face the householders who, to be fair, gave me nothing but encouragement and support – I even thought of waiting with a gun to shoot the damn thing if it dared to show its face!

But don't worry, like Sir Moris's dragon the mole put up a tremendous fight but I caught him in the end and now the residents around Burley Beacon can sleep easily, once again, in their beds.

Oh, by the way it wasn't just big it was enormous!

November

When is a bottom not a bottom? Or, to put it more succinctly, when is a bottom not that part of your anatomy upon which you sit? I can answer this conundrum for you with the voice of bitter experience; it's when a bottom is a bog or a mire and this can be especially relevant when you're in one up to your bottom – yes, the bit you sit on – slowly but surely sinking and fervently praying that your feet will find a hard bottom – nothing to do with the bit you sit on - before the water level reaches the top of your head.

I speak of course about the many bottoms that abound across this beautiful New Forest of ours and which form the backbone of this unique wetland which is so important in the great, ecological scheme of things. These bottoms come in various forms; some are gentle, grassy lawns sloping down to small, meandering streams; others might be buried in tall, feathery reeds interspersed with the brown, accusing fingers of the reedmace or bulrush; many are impassable bogs, often covered in the deceptive and enticing sphagnum moss which can lure the unwary to a watery end. In some of these deeper mires, tussock grass is abundant and these thick, solid plants that grow well above the surrounding water level can form ready- made 'stepping stones' for those who wish to cross a wetland. But do be careful, for the tops of the tussocks are notoriously uneven and the fringed edges are ill defined; it's very easy to miss your footing and slip down between the tussocks and into the peaty, smelly mire below. At best you might get a wet foot, but more often than not, the legs will disappear up to the aforementioned bottom - the one you sit on - and after easing yourself from the cloying, brown soup you'll make another important discovery which is the tenacity of peat, for it will take a good many washes to obliterate the resultant stains from your trousers!

Now, if you don't fancy a bit of tussock hopping then take out your map instead and just look at some of the fascinating place names that these bottoms have given us. In an idle moment I did just that and I managed to find about fifty, named bottoms. Withybed, Broomy, Appleslade, Alderhill, Two Beeches, Broad Oak, Yew Tree and Dogwood Bottoms all speak for themselves. But what secrets or mysteries lie behind the names of Horse Shoe, Horse Bush, Shatterford and Foulford Bottom? Buckherd and Crow's Nest Bottom conjure images of days long gone; whilst

Deadman and Black Gutter Bottom seem almost ominous in origin. There are one or two that, clearly, have more specific but unknown beginnings; what about Rakes Brakes bottom and Strodgemoor Bottom? And, I have to say, the idea of Scrape Bottom brings tears to my eyes! My two favourite names, however, are right here on the outskirts of our village. Close by to Burbush car park we have Slap Bottom and on the right hand side of Station Road as you drive toward the tea rooms is Anthony's Bee Bottom!

A New Forest bottom

On a more serious note, these bottoms are the homes of many rare and endangered plant, animal and insect species and it's essential that they are preserved for the future. Fortunately, their very nature keeps invading footfall to a minimum but they are delicate environments which can easily be damaged by careless actions.

Must go now before I too get a slapped bottom!

December

Boxing Day, as some of you will know, is a Red-Letter day in the countryman's' calendar and here, in the New Forest, many will attend both the fox hound meet and the annual New Forest point-to-point; but, if you could travel back in time on this auspicious day, you might well find yourself witnessing a long-lost, Christmas tradition - **The Great Squirrel Hunt.** Squirrel or 'Skuggie' hunting has been a popular and essential Forest sport for centuries. Squirrels are the number one public enemy of woodmen and arboriculturists and consequently they have been relentlessly persecuted since the instigation of commercial woodlands. Contrary to popular belief, squirrel meat is succulent and nourishing and our poor forebears, who invariably had many mouths to feed, were always eager to help with the relentless fight to keep the numbers of squirrels under control. It is not surprising, therefore, that when the less-fortunate set-out to celebrate Boxing Day they chose to follow a sport that suited their pockets and at which they showed the greatest of skill.

So, early in the morning, large gatherings of men assembled from each Forest village and, often accompanied by a cart filled with bread, cheese and, of course, beer to lift their sprits, they set-out into the bare woodlands to go *Squoyling*; the object of which was to slay as many Skuggies as they could before dusk. There was great rivalry between these gangs of hunters whose sole aim was to return to their local hostelry with the greatest number of beasts, which were duly transformed by the landlady, whilst the hunters relaxed over a pint or two in front of a roaring log fire, into a huge pie that would be devoured later that evening during the celebrations. It has been recorded that bags in excess of one hundred skuggies were not uncommon; and it was the native red squirrel they hunted not the grey immigrant of today that at that time in history was still tucked-up in its native North America and where many wish it had remained!

So how did a band of impoverished Foresters manage to harvest such large numbers of skuggies in such a short period of time? Shooting them with expensive cartridges was not an option. Instead they used the most basic weapon known to mankind; a weapon that required far more skill than the simplest of guns – the throwing stick.

Two distinct types of these lethal throwing sticks were employed and well preserved examples can be seen in the New Forest museum in Lyndhurst. The *Squoyle, Squail or Scale* was made from a slightly-flexible stick, twelve to fifteen inches long with a head of hard wood whilst the *Snog* which had a thicker, wooden shaft was weighted at one end by a lump of lead.

The old Foresters must have been extremely skilled in the use of these missiles and, the Hon. Gerald Lascelles, who retired as Deputy Surveyor in 1915 and who was himself a great, sporting man writes that '*to see them fetch a squirrel out of the tops of the highest branches, sometimes as he bounds from one branch to another, or again as he flattens himself for concealment against the trunk of the tree at ninety feet up, is a perfect revelation.*'

The Snog

Despite evidence of letters of objection from 'Squirrel huggers' around the 1900's, the end of the sport did not come about by pressure from the anti-hunting sector but through the lack of squirrels themselves, possibly from an outbreak of the squirrel pox virus. Sadly, by 1947 the red squirrel had disappeared altogether from the New Forest and, so it seems, did the tradition of Boxing Day squoyling.

The Squoyle, Squail or Scale and Snog

This gives a whole new meaning to 'a quick snog under the mistletoe!'

Merry Christmas.

The other books From a New Forest Inclosure

From A New Forest Inclosure
The First Two Years
Ian Thew

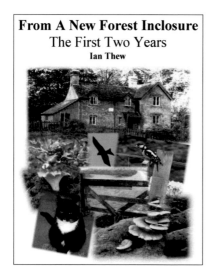

From a New Forest Inclosure
Book Two 2006 & 2007
Ian Tew

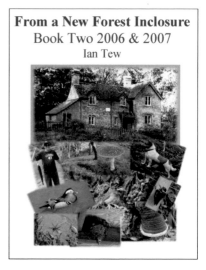

From a New Forest Inclosure
Book Three 2008 & 2009
Ian Thew

From A New Forest Inclosure
Book Four 2010 & 2011
Ian Thew

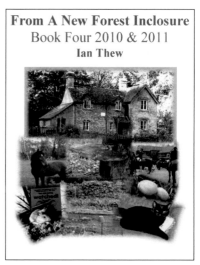

These books are available by post: Please send £5,99 per book plus £2.50 postage and packaging (up to four books) to Ian Thew, Burley Rails Cottage, Burley BH24 4HT England Or telephone 01425 403735 with your name, postal address and card details. Email ian@ithew.freeserve.co.uk

Burley Rails Cottage, Wilfs Cabin and Paddocks

Wilfs Cabin

Stables

Wilfs Cabin; a self-contained, snug, traditional log cabin that provides a double bed room with en-suite shower, a cosy lounge and a galley kitchen. The timbered veranda is ideal for alfresco dining or for just relaxing with a glass of wine after a busy day in the Forest.

For the four legged visitors there are two, modern, block-built, stables with individual yards and a tack room with all facilities, which are adjacent to two small turn-out paddocks. There is ample parking and undercover storage for traps and bikes.

www.burleyrailscottage.co.uk   Tel:01425 403735

Well behaved and sociable dogs are also welcome.

NEW FOREST
Shooting & Fishing | Coaching & Tuition

The New Forest Fly Fishing and Shooting School was founded by Ian Thew who lives deep in the heart of the New Forest which is situated on the South Coast between the mighty rivers Test and Avon and offers the ultimate in fishing and shooting possibilities.

Our objective is to provide the very best in fly fishing and clay and game shooting for both the complete novice or the experienced sportsman and to this end we extend the opportunity to learn new skills or to hone existing expertise over a wide range of disciplines.

We take pride in providing instruction and coaching in all aspects of fishing and shooting to the very highest of standards and we take care to ensure that when our pupils leave us they will have been well versed in both safety and etiquette and will thus be able to move on in their selected sport with personal assurance and confidence.

Ian Thew is a qualified fly fishing coach and a qualified shooting instructor and, in addition to running the New Forest Fly Fishing and Shooting School, he writes regular features on all aspects of shooting, fishing and country sports related topics for magazines such as the Shooting Times and the Countrymans' weekly.

Ian is also a qualified deer stalker and over the past forty years he has amassed a unique and widespread knowledge of most rural activities from fishing to ferreting and just about everything else in between.

Contact Ian on 01425 403735 or email ian@ithew.freeserve.co.uk

www.shootingandfishingcoaching.co.uk

58